427
BAS

LEGE LEARNING CEN

Business
English Words

David Eastment

D1332805

Lowlands Road, Harrow
Middx HA1 3AQ
020 8909 6520

PENGUIN E

HARROW COLLEGE

077221

Pearson Education Limited
Edinburgh Gate
Harlow
Essex CM20 2JE, England
and Associated Companies throughout the world.

ISBN 978-0-582-46885-6

First published 2001
Sixth impression 2008
Text copyright © David Eastment 2001

The moral right of the author has been asserted.

Produced for the publisher by Bluestone Press, Charlbury, UK
Designed and typeset by White Horse Graphics, Charlbury, UK
Illustrations by Anthony Seldon (Graham-Cameron Illustration)
Photography by Patrick Ellis
Printed and bound in China. (EPC/06)

*All rights reserved; no part of this publication may be reproduced, stored in a
retrieval system, or transmitted in any form or by any means, electronic,
mechanical, photocopying, recording or otherwise, without the prior written
permission of the Publishers.*

Published by Pearson Education Limited in association with
Penguin Books Ltd, both companies being subsidiaries of Pearson plc.

The companies referred to in this book are fictitious; any resemblance to real
companies is unintentional.

For a complete list of the titles available from Penguin English visit
our website at www.penguinenglish.com, or please write to your local
Pearson Education office or to: Penguin English Marketing Department,
Pearson Education, Edinburgh Gate, Harlow, Essex CM20 2JE.

Contents

3

Getting
started

Why business words?

As a business person, it is very likely that you will need to use English sometimes at work.

What's in this book?

There are over 250 really useful English words. Each chapter looks at a different area of business life – for example, finance, products and services, sales and marketing. At the end of every chapter you'll find exercises to help you remember what you've learned. And you can check your answers at the back of the book. All the words in the book are also listed in the **Index**.

Why is this book called a *Quick Guide*?

Because it takes you straight to the words you need. For instance, everyone involved in business needs to be able to refer to their own and other companies and organisations. So why not turn to the first chapter, *Company profiles*, starting on page 11? You will find that all the words in this chapter are immediately useful to you.

This is a *Quick Guide*. You don't need to spend hours studying it. Just open it for ten minutes every day – and see how quickly you learn.

- Choose a subject that interests you. Maybe your job involves selling. Look at chapter 4, *Sales and marketing*. Read the chapter and see how many of the words you already know, and how many are new to you.

- Answer the questions in the **Review** section at the end of the chapter. Then go to the **Answers** at the back of the book. Were you right?

- Now go to the **Index**. Read the sample sentences – and write down the words in your own language.

I hope you enjoy using the book. Good luck!

Company
profiles

1

Sole trader

As a taxi driver, I have to keep working even when I'm on holiday!

I'm **self-employed**. I set up my **company** over 25 years ago. I started small and I've stayed small. But I've kept my prices low, and I've kept my **customers** happy. I get lots of repeat business. I've done pretty well.

I haven't got many **overheads**. I don't need an office, just my car and a mobile phone.

I've got no **employees**, I work alone. No meetings, no problems. Holidays? No, no holidays. I have to keep working. Who's going to run the business while I am away?

self-employed

company

customer

overheads

employee

Dot.com companies

THE WORLD'S **BIGGEST** ONLINE COMPUTER GAMES RETAILER

THE HOME OF THE WORLD'S BIGGEST COMPUTER GAMES RETAILER

On the Net, nobody knows how big your company is.

A **dot.com** company can be started with very little money. You don't need much **capital** – just a computer, an Internet connection ... and a good idea. On the Net, nobody knows how big your company is.

All **trading** carries some risk. But **e-commerce** – doing business on the Net – is especially risky. Everything is new – the technology, the customers, the business model. The new dot.com **entrepreneurs**, mostly in their twenties, are ready to take these risks. For them, trading **online** is the future – and it's fun.

dot.com

capital

trading

e-commerce

entrepreneur

online

The supermarket

*... they want high-quality personal **service**.*

The multinational

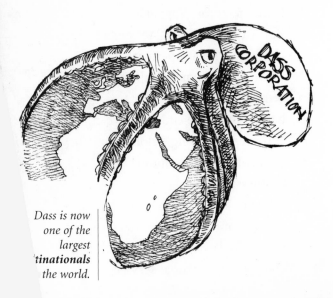

Dass is now one of the largest 'tinationals the world.

A: I see they're opening a new supermarket next month.

B: Yes.

A: Good news for shoppers.

B: But bad news for us. We can't **compete** with a supermarket. We're just too small. Half the **retailers** in town will be **bankrupt** by the end of the year.

A: You're exaggerating. I don't think many of us will go out of business.

B: Why not?

A: Because our customers prefer us. It's not low prices they want, it's high-quality personal **service**.

compete

retailer

bankrupt

service

Andrew Dass started Dass Corporation in the early seventies. He put together computers in his garage and sold them to friends and neighbours. Two years later, he opened his first shop. Within five years, he owned **retail outlets** throughout North America.

In 1980, Dass merged with Gill plc. The **merger** made Dass the sixth biggest **manufacturer** of computers in the USA. In the next ten years, they opened **factories** in Europe, Asia and South America.

Dass is now one of the largest **multinationals** in the world, with offices in over 130 countries. The garage is now part of the Andrew Dass Museum.

retail outlet

merger

manufacturer

factory

multinational

Ask the expert

If business is bad, you may have to sell your house ...

Ask the Expert

Q: I want to start my own business as a computer consultant. What kind of company should I set up?

A: In Britain, if it's just you, the easiest is to be a **sole trader**. No legal problems, no bureaucracy. You are self-employed. If you're planning to work with one or two others, you could form a **partnership**. Partners share the risks, and the profits.

But a sole trader and a partnership have **liability** for **debts**. If business is bad, you may have to sell your house! That's why some people set up a **limited company**. It is easier to borrow money, and even if you go out of business, your home is safe.

sole trader

partnership

liability

debt

limited company

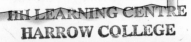

LEARNING CENTRE
HARROW COLLEGE

Review 1

A Fill in the missing words.

1 He keeps his prices down by keeping his o.... low.
2 Most trading in the future will be done o...., using the Internet.
3 She keeps starting new businesses. She's a real e..... .

B Match 1–3 with a–c.

1 self-employed   a) retail outlet
2 online trading   b) sole trader
3 shop   c) e-commerce

C Choose the correct word.

1 All partners have *reliability/liability* for their business debts.
2 Following the *merger/margin*, the two companies were fully integrated.

Joining up

2

Expanding

Wiring the world.

PRESS RELEASE

Futsys Plc is a dynamic new company in the electronics **sector**, with a **workforce** of over 400 in London and the South East. The company had a **turnover** of £150 million last year.

Futsys is now planning to expand into Europe. In the coming year, 12 new **posts** will be created in its **sales** department, based in Central London.

Futsys: Wiring the World!

sector

workforce

turnover

post

sales

Recruiting

Marketing Assistant

WE are specialists in home and garden furniture, with shops throughout the European Union. We now have a **vacancy** for a marketing assistant to work at our Head Office in Paris.

YOU will have a **background** in the **retail** sector, and an interest in foreign languages.

Interviews will be held in London at the end of the month.

For more information, contact John Dyce on 555-0202.

vacancy

background

retail

interview

Job description

Position: Customer Services Manager

Reports to: Head of Customer Services

position

report to

responsibility

supervise

Responsibilities:
- **Supervise** all secretaries and receptionists;
- Participate in all meetings;
- Write company newsletter;
- Meet all visitors and guests;
- Pour coffee.

*The Customer Services Manager has many **responsibilities**.*

The right person

*On the other hand, he is the **MD**'s son …*

A: He has no **qualifications**. He left school at 16.

B: And very little **experience**. He hasn't had a job since he left school.

A: How about **motivation**?

B: He hasn't asked a single question. I don't think he has even read the **job description**! And as for personality …

A: I know. He hasn't smiled once.

A: On the other hand, he is the **MD's*** son …

qualification

experience

motivation

job description

MD

---

* Managing Director

Valuing staff

*Show them that you **value** them.*

Ask the Expert

Q: I find it easy to **recruit** staff, I just can't keep them. Any ideas?

A: People always think that all you need is a high **salary** and good **perks**. But money and benefits are not enough these days. You need to give all your employees interesting, **challenging** work. Encourage them to develop new skills. Give them a chance to learn. But most of all, show them that you **value** them.

recruit

salary

perk

challenging

value

Review 2

A Match 1–3 with a–c.

1 background   a) position
2 post ✓   b) staff
3 workforce   c) experience

B Find four more words in the grid.

P	D	V	A	R	S	R	O
E	X	A	C	T	Q	E	I
R	E	C	R	U	I	T	K
K	O	A	E	J	U	A	D
S	I	N	S	Z	O	I	T
C	C	C	T	D	D	L	D
W	E	Y	I	P	O	S	T

C Fill in the gaps with words from this chapter.

1 The company had a t.... of £500,000 last year.
2 He left school with no q..... No wonder he can't find a job.
3 They are holding i.... for the new job today.

Review 2

A Match 1–3 with a–c.

1 background   a) position
2 post ✓   b) staff
3 workforce   c) experience

B Find four more words in the grid.

P	D	V	A	R	S	R	O
E	X	A	C	T	Q	E	I
R	E	C	R	U	I	T	K
K	O	A	E	J	U	A	D
S	I	N	S	Z	O	I	T
C	C	C	T	D	D	L	D
W	E	Y	I	P	O	S	T

Fill in the gaps with words from this chapter.

The company had a t.... of £500,000 last year.

He left school with no q..... No wonder he can't find a job.

They are holding i.... for the new job today.

A: He has no **qualifications**. He left school at 16.

B: And very little **experience**. He hasn't had a job since he left school.

A: How about **motivation**?

B: He hasn't asked a single question. I don't think he has even read the **job description**! And as for personality …

A: I know. He hasn't smiled once.

A: On the other hand, he is the **MD's*** son …

qualification

experience

motivation

job description

MD

* Managing Director

Valuing staff

*Show them that you **value** them.*

Ask the Expert

Q: I find it easy to **recruit** staff, I just can't keep them. Any ideas?

A: People always think that all you need is a high **salary** and good **perks**. But money and benefits are not enough these days. You need to give all your employees interesting, **challenging** work. Encourage them to develop new skills. Give them a chance to learn. But most of all, show them that you **value** them.

recruit

salary

perk

challe

value

Products
and
services

3

Production

RETRAINING

*The new **facility** will allow the company to reduce its workforce.*

Doyogo Inc. has an international reputation for its electronic **products**. The company has now introduced a new **production line** for computer monitors in its Tokyo **plant**. The line will increase production **capacity** by 50%.

The new **facility** will allow the company to reduce its workforce by 10%. The employees will be offered work in other departments.

product

production line

plant

capacity

facility

Health and safety

*We pay great attention to **safety**.*

Assembly

The only human being is Janice …

We pay great attention to the
safety of all our employees.
We have the latest **equipment**,
and all of it is checked every
month. In fact, we have a
maintenance staff of over 20,
and two full-time safety officers.

All our **procedures** are written
down. We keep notes on
everything we do, and how we
do it. And we keep records of
everything that happens in the
workplace.

Of course, accidents still
happen …

safety

equipment

maintenance

procedure

workplac

And here, ladies and gentlemen, is our **assembly line**. We used to have 100 **unskilled** workers. Now we use robots. We believe that we are industry leaders in **automation**. The only human being in this part of the plant is Janice, who is responsible for the **quality control** of the finished products. When each item has been checked, it is sent on for **packing** …

assembly line

unskilled

automation

quality control

packing

Services

Remember, the customer is always right.

We are a small **consultancy** working in all areas of the **leisure** industry. We offer a range of services, including training, advice and market information. In our **state-of-the-art** computer facilities we offer computer-based **courses** in foreign languages, computer skills, and hotel management.

For further information, please contact …

consultancy

leisure

state-of-the-art

course

Just in time

*Just in Time avoids holding too much **stock**.*

Ask the Expert

Q: What is JIT and why is it important?

A: JIT means *Just in Time*. The old way of manufacturing was to guess the **demand** for a product. Then you made the products, and put them in a **warehouse** until your sales staff could sell them. With JIT, you wait until something is actually needed. You need a lot of **flexibility** from your workforce. It is much more efficient, and avoids holding too much **stock**.

demand

warehouse

flexibility

stock

Review 3

A Match 1–3 with a–c.

1 production   a) plant
2 factory   b) modern
3 state-of-the-art   c) manufacturing

B Replace the words in italics.

1 It is difficult to know *how many people want* this product.
2 He is responsible for *making sure things are in good working order.*
3 Everyone should be worried about safety in the *place where you work.*

C What is being described?

1 free-time, non-working time
2 a company which looks at a problem and gives advice
3 a set of instructions for doing something

Sales
and
marketing

4

The salesman

*I love **closing** a sale.*

Michael Mayer has worked in sales since he left school. At first he was a **sales representative** for a camera manufacturer. Then he worked in Europe and the States, specialising in **promotion** and won the *Salesman of the Year* award in 1992. He is now Sales Director for the same company he started with.

'I love it. I love the travel. I love the **negotiations**. And most of all, I love **closing a sale**.'

sales representative

promotion

negotiation

close a sale

Sales

There have been problems with the **launch** of Doyogo's new computer monitor.

Doyogo Inc., the Japanese electronics company, has announced a sharp **downturn** in sales in the last quarter. A spokesman said 'We are disappointed by the fall in sales. However, the strong yen is a problem for all companies in the sector. We expect a significant **increase** in sales in the pre-Christmas period.'

Market **analysts** are not so sure. There have been problems with the **launch** of Doyogo's new computer monitor, and the advertising **campaign** has had little impact.

downturn
increase
analyst
launch
campaign

Launching a
product

*We may have problems with **transportation**.*

INTERNAL MEMO

To:	Sales and Marketing Staff
From:	Head of Sales and Marketing
Subject:	Meeting: 10 January

Congratulations to all of you on meeting your sales **targets** for Quarter 3. We now need to meet to plan a **strategy** to promote our newest product, the QT-3486. We will need to **brainstorm** pricing and promotion. I would also like to discuss **distribution** – the QT is a big product, and we may have problems with **transportation**. Ideas for a better name than QT-3486 will also be welcome!

target

strategy

brainstorm

distribution

transportation

Branding

But how do you clean your teeth with it?

A: What is your most successful **brand**?

B: Mazat. The chocolate. We've just finished a major **survey** of our products. Mazat had more **brand recognition** than anything else. We mailed out 5,000 **questionnaires**. We did interviews in the street. We put a **poll** on our website. Over 69% of the people we asked had heard of Mazat.

A: So you should be happy!

B: Yes, I should. But most people thought it was a brand of toothpaste …

brand

survey

brand recognition

questionnaire

poll

Getting it right

It has to be in the best location.

Review 4

A Match 1–4 with a–d.

1 rise   a) location
2 downturn   b) increase
3 place   c) salesperson
4 representative   d) fall

B Fill in the gaps with words from this chapter.

1 His shop was too small, so he decided to move to new p.....
2 Coca Cola is a famous b.....
3 Advertising c.... can include television, newspapers, posters and many other media.

C Choose the correct word.

The *launch/lunch* of the new model has been a great success.
Perfume usually has a high profit *merger/margin*.

Ask the Expert

Q: I'm starting a new business, selling musical instruments. How should I **market** myself?

A: You have to think about the four Ps! The first two are the *product* and the *price* you sell it at. Are you selling expensive instruments with high profit **margins**, or are you aiming for **bulk** sales? Then think about how you *promote* your shop. How will people know about it? Where will you place **advertisements**? But the most important thing is *place*. You have to get the right **premises**. You have to get people into your shop, and it has to be in the best location.

market

margin

bulk

advertisemen

premises

Finance

5

Figures

BOARD ROOM

PROFITS

*But we won't have to pay any **tax** ...*

The latest **figures** from our **accountant** show that we earned £2 million in the last financial year. An **income** of £2 million is much better than we expected, and I congratulate our marketing people. In the same period, however, our **expenditure** rose. We needed to employ a large number of extra staff. In fact, our expenditure increased to £2.5 million. That's the bad news. The good news is that we will not have to pay any **tax** …

figures

accountant

income

expenditure

tax

Cashflow

He used his house as **collateral**.

A: This is serious. We've run out of cash.

B: But we have plenty of business!

A: Yes, but no-one has paid us yet.

B: I see. Another **cashflow** problem. What about asking the bank?

A: We have already gone over our **overdraft** limit.

B: How about a **loan**?

A: We'll need some sort of **collateral**. No-one is going to give us an **unsecured** loan.

B: Well, there's always your new house …

cashflow

overdraft

loan

collateral

unsecured

Exchange

We've won the **contract**.

MEMO

To:	Managing Director
From:	Chief Financial Officer

I understand that we have been successful in winning the **contract** with Smithson in Hawaii. Any **export** order is good news, of course. With an **exchange rate** of $1.60 to the pound, it is very good news. But I must advise you that **payment** is not due until the end of next year, and that we are **invoicing** in US currency. If the dollar continues to strengthen, we will have a serious problem on our hands. Please can we speak urgently?

contract

export

exchange rate

payment

invoice

Troubles

They were unable to reach him.

Dear Mr Jones,

In April you took out a Small Business Loan at a fixed **rate** of 6.9%.

You have now missed the last three payments on this loan. We have tried to contact you several times, but have been unable to reach you. It is urgent that you now get in touch with us immediately. As you know, your loan is **secured** on your home. If you do not act at once, we will be forced to consider **foreclosing** on your **mortgage**.

We look forward to hearing from you.

rate

secured

foreclose

mortgage

Credit cards

Do you need a credit card at all?

Ask the Expert

Q: Should I transfer all my credit card debt onto a single card?

A: In theory, yes, you should save money. But you need to be careful when you **consolidate** your debts. Some cards offer a low **interest rate** when you transfer your **balances**, but after six months the rate can go sky high.

Think carefully – do you need a credit card at all? Consider taking out a bank loan to **clear** all your borrowing on cards.

consolidate

interest rate

balance

clear

Review 5

A Fill in the gaps with words from this chapter.

1 This invoice is due for .... within 30 days.
2 What sort of .... can you provide to secure the loan?
3 I'm no good at figures – we'll need to get an .... to calculate our profit.

B Match 1–3 with a–c.

1 The loan is secured   a) by 40%.
2 Payment is due   b) on my home.
3 Expenditure has risen   c) next month.

C Find a business word which means:

1 to put all your loans together: c....
2 the amount of money in an account: b....
3 the money which is owed: d....

More finance

6

Looking ahead

TODAY'S WEATHER

*Of course,
we don't
always get it
right …*

Early this year, Dyled introduced their latest sports car, a hi-tech machine at a reasonable price. Industry analysts loved it. They **forecast** a sharp increase in **profits** for Dyled. Turnover was expected to double in the first year. But things have gone badly wrong. There have been major problems with exports, particularly in the difficult US market. Most experts now expect Dyled to make a **loss** of at least a million over the next year.

Analyst George Burns commented 'We don't always get it right.'

forecast

profit

loss

Insurance

Can you afford *not* to have **insurance**?

A: We rely too much on one or two people in our company. If Steve Jones in engineering had an accident, it would be a disaster for us.

B: Have you heard about Key Person **insurance**? You could take out **cover** against the sickness or death of the most important people in the company.

A: I don't think we could afford the **premiums**.

B: You can pay by monthly **instalments** instead of paying one **lump sum**. Can you afford *not* to have insurance?

insurance

cover

premium

instalment

lump sum

Online trading

Have you thought about trading online?

Are *you* paying your **broker** too much? Have you thought about trading online? You can buy **shares** instantly, and **fees** are tiny compared with what you would pay a broker. At cheaposhares.com, you'll get news. You'll get advice. And best of all, you'll get information. All the information you need to make sure that *your* **portfolio** is delivering what you want.

**Visit us now at
www.cheaposhares.com.
We're only a click away.**

broker

shares

fee

portfolio

Business ethics

PoCo Bank has a new ethical policy on **investment**.

PoCo Bank has announced a new policy on **investment**.

- It will not provide **finance** to companies that damage the environment.

- It will not use its own money to **speculate** against the national currency.

- It will not **lend** to tobacco companies.

- It *will* actively use its **funds** to support companies with a similar philosophy.

investment

finance

speculate

lend

funds

Bank accounts

Dilys, do you know anything about this payment?

Dear Sirs,

I have just received my monthly **bank statement**.

I was surprised to see that £1,200 has been **credited** to our **account** from a company in the United States. And I was shocked to see that you have **debited** our account with £4,600 for a **banker's draft**, which seems to be payable to the same company.

As you know, my business is only local. I have never had any contact with any person or company anywhere in the US.

I look forward to hearing from you.

J. Butcher

bank
statement

credit

account

debit

banker's
draft

Review 6

A Fill in the missing words.

1 He made a lot of money by s.... against the dollar.
2 I try to balance all the shares in my p.....
3 We will c.... your account with the money we owe you.

B Match 1–4 with a–d.

1 banker's   a) statement
2 insurance   b) draft
3 bank   c) sum
4 lump   d) cover

C Find a business word which means …

1 an agent for buying shares
2 a charge for a professional service
3 the amount paid for an insurance policy

Presenting

7

Conferences

BUSINESS ETHICS

A KEY ISSUE

*We are expecting a large number of **participants**.*

INTERNATIONAL CONFERENCE ON BUSINESS ETHICS

This three-day **conference** will be held at Rogers Business School on 17–18 May. The theme of the conference will be 'Ethics – a key issue in today's business world'.

There will be two **plenaries** each day in the Main Hall, with space for up to 500, as well as smaller **workshops** for groups of up to 20. We are expecting a large number of **participants**: early booking is advised!

conference

ethics

plenary

workshop

participant

Giving a
presentation

*And a
computer?*

A: Is everything ready for the meeting? Everyone's here.

B: Yes. I've got my **presentation** on a disk. I've got all the figures we need, and some good **charts** showing sales projections.

A: **Flipchart**?

B: Yes, with plenty of paper. And lots of **handouts**, all photocopied.

A: And a computer?

B: Oh …

presentation

chart

flipchart

handout

Meetings

I'd like to finish before lunch.

I hope you have all had a chance to look through the **agenda**. I have the **minutes** of our last meeting with me. Sorry they are so late!

You have all the **documentation** for each item on the agenda in front of you. I'm going to ask Jane to **chair** the meeting, and I'd like to finish before lunch.

agenda

minutes

documentation

chair

Planning

I would like to demonstrate our new security procedures.

MEMO

To:	All Head Office Staff
Subject:	Training

1. There will be a meeting of all staff next Wednesday at 09:30 to discuss our new security procedures.
2. The **implementation** of the security **initiative** is critical to our success, and it is vital that all staff attend.
3. We need to agree a **timescale**, and to make sure that our planning is completed **on schedule**. Please bring your diaries!

implementation

initiative

timescale

on schedule

Effective talks

Make sure your audience laugh at least once.

OUR FOUNDER

Ask the Expert

Q: What is the secret of giving a good **talk**?

A: That's easy! You just have to remember ABC.

Accuracy – you must get your facts right.

Brevity – keep to the point, and don't use ten words if you can use one.

Clarity – make sure the structure of your talk is clear.

Oh, and make sure your **audience** laugh at least once.

talk

accuracy

brevity

clarity

audience

Review 7

A Which of these are objects you might find in an office?

audience   flipchart   handout   plenary
chart   initiative

B Write the noun from the adjective.

1	accurate	
2	brief	
3	clear	

C Find a business word which means these things.

1 making something happen
2 the order of items in a meeting
3 the written record of a meeting
4 a meeting at a conference which is open to all

Organisations

8

Branch closure

I prefer to do my banking from home.

SFX Bank today announced the **closure** of ten **branches** in Western Europe. SFX will stay in High Street banking but 'is responding to changes in the banking industry caused by new technology. Our customers prefer to do their banking from home.' SFLET, a **subsidiary** of SFX, has an increasing **share** of the market for online banking.

closure
branch
subsidiary
share

Monopoly

DATACOMP is planning a takeover of Itek.

QUESTIONS OVER DATACOMP TAKEOVER

The government has appointed a **commission** to examine the planned **takeover** of Itek Ltd by DATACOMP plc. DATACOMP is a major US **conglomerate** with international interests, and Itek is one of its key **competitors**.

Analysts believe that the proposed company may have a **monopoly** in several key markets, especially in Europe.

commission

takeover

conglomerate

competitor

monopoly

Hierarchies

ME

SUPERVISORS

WORKERS

*We don't believe in **hierarchies**.*

We don't believe in **hierarchies** in this organisation. We've only got three **layers**: workers, **supervisors**, and me. There are no departmental heads reporting to a **board of directors**. We don't have departments, we have business units. And we don't have any **shareholders**, either. It's my company, and I run it how I want.

hierarchy

layer

supervisor

board of directors

shareholder

Franchises

*A unique **opportunity** to grow your own business.*

FRANCHISE OPPORTUNITY

Do you have £10,000 to invest in a new business? Have you thought about a **franchise**? We are a major **corporation** specialising in domestic goods. We offer a unique **opportunity** for you to grow your own successful business. We offer full support to our **franchisees**, including advice and high-quality promotional materials.

franchise

corporation

opportunity

franchisee

Business links

*There was no alternative to **acquisition**.*

When my company – Small & Co. – started working with BNR, it started out as just a normal trading **relationship**. Then our **association** got closer and closer. We formed a strategic **alliance**. We operated **nationwide**: they had the south, I had the north. But they were much bigger than me. In the end, there was no alternative to **acquisition** – they bought me out for a lot of money.

relationship

association

alliance

nationwide

acquisition

Review 8

A Fill in the gaps with words from this chapter.

1 KFC and McDonald's are both .... operations.

2 We operate in every part of the country. We are truly .....

3 Managers should look after the interests of their .....

B Put these words into two groups: people and companies.

shareholder   branch   subsidiary
franchisee   conglomerate   supervisor

C Find a business word which means ...

1 the American word for 'company'

2 a situation where a company has no competitors

3 a situation where two companies stay separate, but work closely together

Customers

9

Complaints

I am writing to express my **dissatisfaction**.

Dear Sirs,

I am writing, for the third time, to express my **dissatisfaction** with the service I have received from your company.

The details of my **complaint** are in my letter of 5 March. You replied with a copy of your policy on **customer care**, but did not answer any of my questions.

Your product has so far cost me several thousand dollars. I look forward to hearing what you have to say about **compensation**.

Yours faithfully

J. Savage

dissatisfaction

complaint

customer care

compensation

Procedures

*Damage to **components** has occurred during packing.*

MEMO

To:	*All staff*
Subject:	*Complaints*

Unfortunately, we are receiving a large volume of complaints regarding the FL-9000. **Defects** *have been found at the manufacturing stage and some* **damage** *to* **components** *has occurred during packing. We urgently need to look into these problems. Please attend a meeting in my office at 9 am tomorrow.*

defect

damage

component

Focus groups

The group were happy to participate in the research.

Thank you for coming. The aim of this **focus group** is to get **feedback** from you on our new range of chocolates. We want to hear your **criticisms**, your suggestions, your feelings. You are the real experts, you are the **consumers** – you eat what we make! We want to hear anything about how our products are performing in the **marketplace**. We're not here to talk, just to listen. So please, sit back and relax – and eat!

focus group

feedback

criticism

consumer

marketplace

Loyalty

Benefits
include an
increased
baggage
allowance.

TARIG Air has just announced a new Airmiles program, 'Miles and Smiles'.

Our aim is to increase customer **loyalty**. We want people to fly with us again and again. We believe we offer the best service – and we plan to make it even better.

Passengers who **enrol** on our program will get a wide range of **rewards**, including upgrades, and even free flights. Other **benefits** include fast-track check-in and an increased baggage **allowance**.

loyalty

enrol

reward

benefit

allowance

Customer rights

THE GUARANTEE IS INVALID AFTER YOU OPEN THE BOX

CAMERA   35 mm camera

I don't believe it!

Thank you for purchasing the X6 Digital Camera. Our **guarantee** covers your new camera for one year from the date of purchase. Our relationship with our customers is important to us. Please complete the **registration card** and answer the questions on the enclosed **leaflet**, and send it back to us. Your **incentive**? As soon as we hear from you, we will send you a free book on getting the most out of your new camera.

guarantee

registration card

leaflet

incentive

Review 9

A Fill in the gaps.

1 We need to know what they think. But how can we get ....?

2 They won't reply unless they get something in return. We'll need to offer an .....

3 This product has so many ..... I'm going to send it back to the manufacturer.

B Write the noun from the verb.

1 allow   2 complain   3 criticise

4 consume

C Find a word which means these things.

1 a payment for damage or nuisance: c....

2 protection if something you buy is faulty: g....

3 something which is wrong or faulty: d....

People

10

Careers

*Madeleine started her **career** as an **office junior**.*

Madeleine Stretch started her **career** as an **office junior**. But she didn't make tea and open letters for long. After just a few months, she joined the **personnel** department. After several quick promotions, she became a company director in 1992. Thanks to her **creativity** and her ability to solve problems, she quickly rose to the top. Now, at the age of 46, she is **CEO*** of one of the world's largest multinationals.

career

office junior

personnel

creativity

CEO

*CEO – Chief Executive Officer

Leadership

*My **leadership skills** can save the company.*

I'm not an intellectual. But I have **focus** – I concentrate my energy, and I know where I'm going. I've got **ambition**, but so have all successful business people. What makes me different is that I have **vision** – I know exactly where I want this company to be in five years from now. Most important of all, I can get people to join in my vision. I am a **leader** – and it is my **leadership skills** that can save this company.

focus

ambition

vision

leader

leadership skills

Redundancy

*The workers will get a generous **redundancy** package.*

DAIYO JOBS SHOCK

Following a review of their operations in Asia, Daiyo are restructuring their business. Two factories will be closed, with up to 500 **redundancies**.

'We have consulted closely with the **trade unions**', said a spokesperson. 'We will be forced to **lay off** staff, but are offering retraining and **redeployment** at our other factories wherever possible. All other workers will get a generous redundancy **package**.'

redundancy

trade union

lay off

redeployment

package

Leave

*Please mark your holidays on the **wallchart**.*

MEMO

To:	*All staff*
From:	*MD*
Subject:	*Absence from work*

*Can I please remind all staff that they <u>must</u> mark their **absence** on **leave** or business on the **wallchart** in the front office. Please make sure you submit the correct **form** for my **approval** at least one month before you plan to take your leave.*

absence

leave

wallchart

form

approval

At the office

*She's the
only one
with her
own office.*

A: The **receptionists** are by the door. They welcome **visitors**, and look after the switchboard. Over there are our **secretaries**. Most of them are **temps** from a local agency, except Janet. She's **PA** to the MD.

B: PA to the MD?

A: Sorry, Personal Assistant to the Managing Director.

B: And where is he?

A: She. She's the only one with her own office, over there.

receptionist

visitor

secretary

temp

PA

Review 10

A **Put these words into two groups: people and qualities.**

temp   ambition   leadership   leader
creativity   vision   visitor   receptionist
focus

B **Fill in the gaps with words from this chapter.**

1 He's a natural ..... Everyone is ready to follow him.
2 Where are you going on .... this summer?
3 There were over a hundred .... when they shut down the bank.

C **Write these job titles in full.**

1 MD
2 PA
3 CEO

Index

Your language

absence /ˈæbsəns/
He sent apologies for his absence. _____

account /əˈkaʊnt/
Please settle this account immediately! _____

accountant /əˈkaʊntənt/
My accountant is very efficient. _____

accuracy /ˈækjərəsi/
I doubt the accuracy of this report. _____

acquisition /ˌækwɪˈzɪʃən/
Their new acquisition is a food retailer. _____

advertisement /ədˈvɜːtismənt/
The advertisement appeared yesterday. _____

agenda /əˈdʒendə/
The agenda for this meeting is too long. _____

alliance /əˈlaɪəns/
The two companies formed an alliance. _____

allowance /əˈlaʊəns/
The baggage allowance is 30 kilos. _____

Your language

ambition /æmbɪʃən/
Her ambition is to get to the top. _____

analyst /ænəlɪst/
The analyst will uncover the facts. _____

approval /əpruːvəl/
He did not get his manager's approval. _____

assembly line /əsembli laɪn/
The assembly line stopped for repairs. _____

association /əsəʊsieɪʃən/
Our association started in May. _____

audience /ɔːdiəns/
He always keeps his audience interested. _____

automation /ɔːtəmeɪʃən/
Automation often means job losses. _____

background /bækgraʊnd/
His background is in sales. _____

balance /bæləns/
What is the balance on my account? _____

Your language

banker's draft /bæŋkəz drɑːft/
I plan to pay by banker's draft. _____

bankrupt /bæŋkrʌpt/
Unfortunately, he went bankrupt. _____

bank statement /bæŋk steɪtmənt/
I checked my bank statement for errors. _____

benefit /benɪfɪt/
Our staff benefits include free coffee. _____

board of directors
/bɔːd əv dərektəz/
The board of directors will decide. _____

brainstorm /breɪnstɔːm/
We are going to brainstorm solutions. _____

branch /brɑːntʃ/
They are opening a branch in Paris. _____

brand /brænd/
Our brand is recognised worldwide. _____

Your language

brand recognition
/brænd rekəgnıʃən/
Brand recognition is important to us. _____

brevity /brevəti/
The brevity of his talk was welcome. _____

broker /brəʊkə/
I got my insurance through a broker. _____

bulk /bʌlk/
We saved money by buying in bulk. _____

campaign /kæmpeɪn/
The recruitment campaign succeeded. _____

capacity /kəpæsəti/
We increased our production capacity. _____

capital /kæpɪtəl/
I had no capital so I had to borrow. _____

career /kərɪə/
At the age of 40 he changed career. _____

Your language

cashflow /ˈkæʃfləʊ/
Cashflow problems must be avoided. _____

CEO /ˌsiː iː ˈəʊ/
The CEO was popular with his staff. _____

chair /tʃeə/
I will chair today's meeting myself. _____

challenging /ˈtʃælənzɪŋ/
The job is challenging but rewarding. _____

chart /tʃɑːt/
Please mark your holidays on the chart. _____

clarity /ˈklærəti/
His report is a model of clarity. _____

clear /klɪə/
He took out a loan to clear his debts. _____

close a sale /kləʊz ə seɪl/
The representative closed the sale. _____

closure /ˈkləʊʒə/
The firm has been forced into closure. _____

Your language

collateral /kəlætərəl/
You need collateral to borrow money.　　＿＿＿＿＿＿

commission /kəmɪʃən/
The government set up a commission.　　＿＿＿＿＿＿

company /kʌmpəni/
The company is the biggest in Europe.　　＿＿＿＿＿＿

compensation /kɒmpənseɪʃən/
He got compensation for his injury.　　＿＿＿＿＿＿

compete /kəmpiːt/
We cannot compete with them.　　＿＿＿＿＿＿

competitor /kəmpetɪtə/
He is my biggest competitor.　　＿＿＿＿＿＿

complaint /kəmpleɪnt/
They have made a serious complaint.　　＿＿＿＿＿＿

component /kəmpəʊnənt/
This component was made in Korea.　　＿＿＿＿＿＿

conference /kɒnfərəns/
Our annual conference is in Delhi.　　＿＿＿＿＿＿

Your language

conglomerate /kənglɒmərət/
A conglomerate dominated the market. _____

consolidate /kənsɒlədeɪt/
Consolidate borrowing into one loan. _____

consultancy /kənsʌltənsi/
He started a worldwide IT consultancy. _____

consumer /kənsjuːmə/
He was a champion of consumer rights. _____

contract /kɒntrækt/
We've won the contract. _____

corporation /kɔːpəreɪʃən/
Corporations are large businesses. _____

course /kɔːs/
It's a course on designing web pages. _____

cover /kʌvə/
I must get some insurance cover. _____

creativity /kriːeɪtɪvəti/
The agency is noted for its creativity. _____

Your language

credit /ˈkredɪt/
We can't get credit from our suppliers! _____

criticism /ˈkrɪtɪsɪzm/
We take all criticism very seriously. _____

customer /ˈkʌstəmə/
The customer is almost always right. _____

customer care /ˈkʌstəmə keə/
We have a new policy on customer care. _____

damage /ˈdæmɪdʒ/
We apologise for the damage caused. _____

debit /ˈdebɪt/
They debited £1,500 by mistake. _____

debt /det/
They are in debt and cannot pay us. _____

defect /diːˈfekt/
There is a defect in the components. _____

demand /dɪˈmɑːnd/
There is no demand for this product. _____

Your language

dissatisfaction /dɪsætɪsfækʃən/
I want to express my dissatisfaction. _____

distribution /dɪstrəbjuːʃən/
We handle all distribution by rail. _____

documentation /dɒkjʊmənteɪʃən/
This product has no documentation. _____

dot.com /dɒtkɒm/
It's a dot.com specialising in software. _____

downturn /daʊntɜːn/
There is a downturn in the economy. _____

e-commerce /iːkɒmɜːs/
E-commerce is becoming important. _____

employee /emplɔɪi/
The company was bought by employees. _____

enrol /enrəʊl/
You must enrol early for this course. _____

entrepreneur /ɒntrəprənɜː/
He is a famous entrepreneur. _____

Your language

equipment /ɪkwɪpmənt/
Have you checked the new equipment? _____

ethics /eθɪks/
Ethics is important in business. _____

exchange rate /ɪkstʃeɪndʒ reɪt/
What is today's £–$ exchange rate? _____

expenditure /ɪkspendɪtʃə/
Our biggest expenditure is on salaries. _____

experience /ɪkspɪəriəns/
She moved jobs to gain experience. _____

export /ekspɔːt/
This is our most successful export. _____

facility /fəsɪləti/
We opened a new production facility. _____

factory /fæktəri/
This factory provides jobs for the town. _____

fee /fiː/
They have increased their fees by 12%. _____

Your language

feedback /ˈfiːdbæk/
Send us your feedback on our products. _____

figures /ˈfɪɡəz/
The latest figures are not yet available. _____

finance /ˈfaɪnæns/
We'll have to arrange finance for this. _____

flexibility /ˌfleksəˈbɪləti/
His greatest strength is his flexibility. _____

flipchart /ˈflɪptʃɑːt/
He used the flipchart to explain it. _____

focus /ˈfəʊkəs/
The focus has to be on production. _____

focus group /ˈfəʊkəs ɡruːp/
Focus groups helped develop this brand. _____

forecast /ˈfɔːkɑːst/
It can be difficult to forecast demand. _____

foreclose /fɔːˈkləʊz/
The bank foreclosed on her mortgage. _____

Your language

form /fɔːm/
Please fill in the attached form. _____

franchise /fræntʃaɪz/
He runs a fast food franchise operation. _____

franchisee /fræntʃaɪziː/
They have 900 franchisees worldwide. _____

funds /fʌndz/
The bank made funds available at once. _____

guarantee /gærəntiː/
All our products carry a guarantee. _____

handout /hændaʊt/
This handout shows this year's results. _____

hierarchy /haɪrɑːki/
There is a strict hierarchy in the firm. _____

implementation /ɪmpləmenteɪʃən/
Implementation of the rules starts now. _____

incentive /ɪnsentɪv/
We offer bonuses as an incentive. _____

Your language

income /ˈɪnkəm/
Her income has doubled this year. _____

increase /ˈɪnkriːs/
There has been an increase of 50%. _____

initiative /ɪˈnɪʃətɪv/
You need to show more initiative. _____

instalment /ɪnˈstɔːlmənt/
I've paid the last instalment of my loan. _____

insurance /ɪnˈʃʊrəns/
The new factory will need insurance. _____

interest rate /ˈɪntrəst reɪt/
The interest rate is fixed for three years. _____

interview /ˈɪntəvjuː/
We have six candidates to interview. _____

investment /ɪnˈvestmənt/
It was an excellent investment. _____

invoice /ˈɪnvɔɪs/
We'll be invoicing in US currency. _____

Your language

job description /dʒɒb dəskrɪpʃən/
They won't give me a job description. _____

launch /lɔːntʃ/
It's the launch of a new product line. _____

layer /leɪə/
We removed a layer of management. _____

lay off /leɪ ɒf/
We have to lay off some of our staff. _____

leader /liːdə/
She was a great leader. _____

leadership skills /liːdəʃɪp skɪlz/
He lacks the necessary leadership skills. _____

leaflet /liːflət/
This leaflet explains all the details. _____

leave /liːv/
When are you going on leave? _____

leisure /leʒə/
The leisure industry has grown. _____

Your language

lend /lend/
The bank is happy to lend us money. _____

liability /laɪəbɪləti/
We admit full liability for the accident. _____

limited company
/lɪmətəd kʌmpəni/
'Ltd.' shows it's a limited company. _____

loan /ləʊn/
The bank has called in its loan. _____

loss /lɒs/
We've made a bigger loss than expected. _____

loyalty /lɔɪəlti/
You showed great loyalty to the firm. _____

lump sum /lʌmp sʌm/
Payment can be made as a lump sum. _____

maintenance /meɪntənəns/
Equipment maintenance can be costly. _____

Your language

manufacturer /mænjufæktʃərə/
We need a reliable manufacturer. _____

margin /mɑːdʒən/
The margin on this product is small. _____

market /mɑːkət/
There is a huge market for our service. _____

marketplace /mɑːkətpleɪs/
It will not succeed in the marketplace. _____

MD /em diː/
The MD was a popular woman. _____

merger /mɜːdʒə/
He planned a merger of the companies. _____

minutes /mɪnəts/
He'll take the minutes of this meeting. _____

monopoly /mənɒpəli/
Telecommunications is a monopoly. _____

mortgage /mɔːgɪdʒ/
We need to take out a new mortgage. _____

Your language

motivation /məʊtəveɪʃən/
His big family was his motivation! _____

multinational /mʌltɪnæʃənəl/
The multinational has branches in LA. _____

nationwide /neɪʃənwaɪd/
We have offices nationwide. _____

negotiation /nɪgəʊʃieɪʃən/
Our price is not open to negotiation. _____

office junior /ɒfɪs dʒuːnɪə/
The office junior brought in the coffee. _____

online /ɒnlaɪn/
Banking online saves us time. _____

on schedule /ɒn ʃedjuːl/
The launch is on schedule for Monday. _____

opportunity /ɒpətjuːnəti/
It's an opportunity for promotion. _____

overdraft /əʊvədrɑːft/
The bank will not extend our overdraft. _____

Your language

overheads /ˈəʊvəhedz/
Cutting overheads will save us money. _____

PA /piː eɪ/
His PA has worked with him for years. _____

package /ˈpækɪdʒ/
It is a generous redundancy package. _____

packing /ˈpækɪŋ/
Careful packing prevents damage. _____

participant /pɑːˈtɪsəpənt/
The conference had 1,000 participants. _____

partnership /ˈpɑːtnəʃɪp/
Those two are setting up a partnership. _____

payment /ˈpeɪmənt/
Payment of this invoice is overdue. _____

perk /pɜːk/
Free meals are one of the perks. _____

personnel /ˌpɜːsəˈnel/
The office personnel changed often. _____

Your language

plant /plɑːnt/
Our whole plant is outdated. _____

plenary /pliːnəri/
The plenary session was well attended. _____

poll /pəʊl/
The results of the poll surprised us all. _____

portfolio /pɔːtfəʊliəʊ/
He has a wide portfolio of shares. _____

position /pəzɪʃən/
Her position in the company is safe. _____

post /pəʊst/
She returned to her post after sick leave. _____

premises /preməsəz/
Security guards patrol the premises. _____

premium /priːmiəm/
The policy has a high premium. _____

presentation /prezənteɪʃən/
Your presentation was fascinating. _____

Your language

procedure /prəsi:dʒə/
He followed procedures carefully. _____

product /prɒdəkt/
The new product has been launched. _____

production line /prədʌkʃən laɪn/
The production line is very inefficient. _____

profit /prɒfɪt/
Increased costs halved their profits. _____

promotion /prəməʊʃən/
His promotion was well deserved. _____

qualification /kwɒləfəkeɪʃən/
He has no recognised qualification. _____

quality control /kwɒləti kəntrəʊl/
Quality control is a priority here. _____

questionnaire /kwestʃəneə/
Please complete this questionnaire. _____

rate /reɪt/
The loan is fixed at a rate of 7.4%. _____

Your language

receptionist /rɪsepʃənɪst/
Our receptionist looks after visitors. _____

recruit /rɪkruːt/
We use an agency to recruit our staff. _____

redeployment /riːdɪplɔɪmənt/
They offered the workers redeployment. _____

redundancy /rɪdʌndənsi/
Her redundancy was unexpected. _____

registration card
/redʒəstreɪʃən kɑːd/
Please fill in the registration card. _____

relationship /rəleɪʃənʃɪp/
We have a good working relationship. _____

report to /rɪpɔːt tə/
He reports directly to the MD. _____

responsibility /rɪspɒnsəbɪləti/
She has responsibility for marketing. _____

Your language

retail /ˈriːteɪl/
Her business is purely retail. _____

retail outlet /ˈriːteɪl ˈaʊtlət/
They have retail outlets in large cities. _____

retailer /ˈriːteɪlə/
Retailers sell direct to the public. _____

reward /rɪˈwɔːd/
We give customers a range of rewards. _____

safety /ˈseɪfti/
The safety of employees is important. _____

salary /ˈsæləri/
My salary is paid each month. _____

sales /seɪlz/
Sales of the car have been excellent. _____

sales representative
/seɪlz reprɪˈzentətɪv/
She's our best sales representative. _____

Your language

secretary /sekrətəri/
The manager relied on his secretary. _____

sector /sektə/
We're involved in new market sectors. _____

secured /sɪkjʊəd/
The loan is secured on his own home. _____

self-employed /self ɪmplɔɪd/
She left her job and went self-employed. _____

service /sɜːvɪs/
The service they provide is excellent. _____

share /ʃeə/
Their share of the market has declined. _____

shareholder /ʃeəhəʊldə/
Shareholders are allowed to vote. _____

shares /ʃeəz/
He sold all his shares in the company. _____

sole trader /səʊl treɪdə/
As a sole trader, he was in charge. _____

Your language

speculate /spekjuleɪt/
It can be risky to speculate in shares. _____

state-of-the-art /steɪt əv ði ɑːt/
The machinery is state-of-the-art. _____

stock /stɒk/
Some of the stock was damaged by fire. _____

strategy /strætədʒi/
What is your strategy for expanding? _____

subsidiary /səbsɪdiəri/
It is a subsidiary of the main company. _____

supervise /suːpəvaɪz/
I supervise six members of staff. _____

supervisor /suːpəvaɪzə/
The supervisor worried about safety. _____

survey /sɜːveɪ/
I conducted a survey of key markets. _____

takeover /teɪkəʊvə/
We have support for our takeover bid. _____

Your language

talk /tɔːk/
There was a small audience for my talk. _____

target /tɑːgət/
We aim to meet our sales targets. _____

tax /tæks/
All these figures are shown before tax. _____

temp /temp/
She left school and worked as a temp. _____

timescale /taɪmskeɪl/
The timescale for the project is critical. _____

trade union /treɪd juːnjən/
The trade union worked with us. _____

trading /treɪdɪŋ/
The company began trading in 1947. _____

transportation /trænspɔːteɪʃən/
Transportation was a big problem. _____

turnover /tɜːnəʊvə/
Their turnover has grown this year. _____

Your language

unsecured /ʌnsɪkjʊəd/
I took out an unsecured business loan. _____

unskilled /ʌnskɪld/
Unskilled workers earn less than we do. _____

vacancy /veɪkənsi/
We have a vacancy for a receptionist. _____

value /væljuː/
The machinery has decreased in value. _____

vision /vɪʒən/
The MD had a clear vision of the future. _____

visitor /vɪzətə/
Each visitor is given a security badge. _____

wallchart /wɔːltʃɑːt/
The wallchart showed the sales figures. _____

warehouse /weəhaʊs/
We need to enlarge our warehouse. _____

workforce /wɜːkfɔːs/
Their workforce has doubled in size. _____

Your language

workplace /wɜːkpleɪs/
Safety is important in the workplace.   _____

workshop /wɜːkʃɒp/
After his talk, he ran a workshop
for new staff.   _____

Answers

Review 1
A 1 overheads 2 online 3 entrepreneur
B 1b 2c 3a
C 1 liability 2 merger

Review 2
A 1c 2a 3b
B perks vacancy retail recruit
C 1 turnover 2 qualifications 3 interviews

Review 3
A 1c 2a 3b
B 1 the demand for 2 maintenance 3 workplace
C 1 leisure 2 consultancy 3 procedure

Review 4
A 1b 2d 3a 4c
B 1 premises 2 brand 3 campaigns
C 1 launch 2 margin

Review 5
A 1 payment 2 collateral 3 accountant
B 1b 2c 3a
C 1 consolidate 2 balance 3 debt

Review 6

A 1 speculating 2 portfolio 3 credit
B 1b 2d 3a 4c
C 1 broker 2 fee 3 premium

Review 7

A flipchart handout chart
B 1 accuracy 2 brevity 3 clarity
C 1 implementation 2 agenda 3 minutes 4 plenary

Review 8

A 1 franchise 2 nationwide 3 shareholders
B PEOPLE: shareholder, franchisee, supervisor
  COMPANIES: branch, subsidiary, conglomerate
C 1 corporation 2 monopoly 3 alliance

Review 9

A 1 feedback 2 incentive 3 defects
B 1 allowance 2 complaint 3 criticism 4 consumer
C 1 compensation 2 guarantee 3 defect

Review 10

A PEOPLE: temp, leader, visitor, receptionist
  QUALITIES: ambition, leadership, creativity, vision, focus
B 1 leader 2 leave 3 redundancies
C 1 MD – Managing Director 2 PA – Personal Assistant
  3 CEO – Chief Executive Officer